Our loved ones are only
a thought away

By

Tara Coyle

To Karen
lots of
love Luck
&
Laughter
your friend
Tara xx

© 2011 Tara Coyle

ISBN: 978-1-907107-86-3

A CIP catalogue for this book is available from the National Library.

This book was published in cooperation with Choice Publishing & Book Services Ltd, Drogheda, Co Louth, Ireland
Tel: 041 9841551 Email: info@choicepublishing.ie
www.choicepublishing.ie

By John Coyle

8th July 2011

'Our loved ones are only a thought away'...........................

By Medium Tara Coyle.

DEDICATION

Before you read my book. I would like you to take the time to get to know my Mum. Her name is Sylvia McGahon, she is an amazing woman, a devoted mother and wife to my father Barry McGahon. My mother is the reason and inspiration for this book. Throughout my life she has been there for me through my highs and lows, she is a wonderful gifted healer and continues to help many people, she touches the lives of those she meets. My Mum is a very talented artist, and teacher of art. I would like to take this opportunity to thank her for bringing me into this world and to tell her I love her more than life. Love you Mum xxx

By Sylvia McGahon

ACKNOWELEDGEMENTS

There are a few people whom I would like to acknowledge, although there are many more, these are a few. My Grandmother Kitty McGahon, Mary Jerome, My Dad, Barry McGahon, Mum, my sisters Roisin and Emma, and my brother Luke. My husband and soul mate Johnny and my wonderful children, Jonathon, Sean, Leanne and Rachel. To my friends for all the support in my work, International Medium Colin Fry, Lorraine Wright, Natasha De Goede, Lynn McBride, Ellen McBride, Michael Floyd, Nicola Traynor, Heather Evans (Medium), Donna Bracken, Charlene Mc Key, Eugene Garvey (The Phone Shop) and all my dear friends in the spirit circle, and all of my spirit guides whom I will introduce to you and to God for giving me life.

Throughout my life these people have made a difference to my development in more ways than they can imagine. I am proud to have these people in my life and thank them from the bottom of my heart for their understanding and guidance of my spiritual journey. To all those whom I have read for, for believing in me and my work. I am grateful to you all, for the times I have spent with you all, and for the deep and inner emotions and parts of your lives you have shared with me. I would also like for thank the Floyd family for allowing me to include Michael (Mickey) Floyd in my book, and last but not least to the Mckey family, especially Charlene and Ann-Marie.

Tara Coyle

ABOUT ME AND WHO I AM

I am 37 years old, with four wonderful children, married to my soul mate, Johnny Coyle. I was born in Leicester, England, daughter of Barry and Sylvia McGahon. My oldest and lifelong friend is Phaedra Knight (Makepeace), a truly inspiring friend, born with PFFD, (Proximal Femoal Focal Deficiency, this is a failure of the normal development of the proximal (upper) end of the femur (thigh bone). Phaedra proved that there was nothing she couldn't achieve, and to this day remains my friend and always will be an inspiration to me of achieving my goals in life.

From birth, I had always acknowledged spirit children as friends, but never realised, that I should tell my parents at the time or how much a big part of my life this would become. My "imaginary friends", were always with me. I never felt alone, always there to play tea parties with me. In life, I could not ask for better parents, although I did not always talk about my spirit friends. I always felt that Mum understood there was something special about me.

As I was growing up, I wondered how others would view me, with my thoughts of the spirit people, would they see me as different, and how would I be classed? Because of these feelings I remained quiet about my 'imaginary friends', so I would fit in. Later in life I have read about indigo children, these are children who have gone through the same as me. I believe from birth until around 10 or 11, children are very much capable of sensing, feeling or seeing spirit, however, as we get older, we are taught logic, and told it's our imagination, and conforms to what society expects as "normal". I guess I didn't need to be conformed and I come across as unusual, well I'm happy and comfortable with that. However, growing up with these abilities was not the easiest believe me. I hope that by writing this book I can encourage people the same as me to stand up and say it's ok to be different after all God has made us all unique.

BRENDAN IN MY LIFE.

Throughout my life, I have always felt a male spirit around me, which I discovered properly about 13 years ago. He was and is my brother Brendan. The bond I have with Brendan is strong and very special for the simple reason, Brendan travelled to the spirit world from my Mums womb, had he not travelled, I would not be here writing this book, as I was conceived after his passing. Brendan is my strongest guide that works with me, although I have several guides, he is my spirit guide from birth. Brendan watches over me as big brothers do, and has his work cut out for him! I have travelled many roads so far in my life, some of the paths I have taken may not have been the right ones, but as I look back, I believe I travelled these roads to learn and gain experience in order for me to do my readings and understand peoples' emotions. As I read, I can recall the emotions I have experienced in my life, which helps me fully understand how the person sitting across from me feels, as it is important to me to understand and to be a friend and listening ear to those who need to talk.

Mum and I openly speak about Brendan, and one day Mum said she would like to see him at least once. Some years ago Mum and I called to a house, as with most readings Mum would write them down as I read for the person, as sometimes I speak fast and it helps the person recall their readings. In the middle of the reading I became aware of Brendan moving away from me for a little while, suddenly I noticed Mum had stopped writing and was staring out the window with tears in her eyes, it was a very precious moment. Mum said she could see Brendan at the clothes line outside. I looked and there he was, Mum had gotten her wish.

About two months after Mum had seen Brendan, I went to get a birthday present for her, I asked Brendan's help in picking something for her. We went into the local pharmacy, not really knowing what to buy; I was looking at some necklaces on a shelf in a glass cabinet in boxes. One of the boxes fell for no reason; the pharmacist came over to me, opened up the cabinet and put the box firmly back on the shelf again. Again the box fell. I asked the assistant to show me the necklace that was in the box. It was a silver angel; it was the only necklace in the cabinet that was an angel. I decided to get this for Mum. On the day of her birthday, I gave her a card and her present. Before I could say anything at all about the necklace, she looked at me with tears of joy in her eyes and said she knew that Brendan had picked it with me. I didn't realise at the time that we were experiencing telepathy, its where two people don't say anything but know what the other person is thinking.

EARLY DAYS IN IRELAND

When I was living in England, I was surrounded by my Mum's family, Grandad Cyril and Grandmother Mary. My uncles' Michael, Paul and Steve, Aunties Pat and Geraldine, and my precious sister and friend Roisin. While in England I went to playschool, I didn't really want to as I would prefer to be at home with my Mum and Dad, but understand now as a parent they had to work to provide for me, and that's something they always did. I never needed for anything, they taught me love, principles and morals, although later in teenager years principle went out the window for a while! At the age of six, Dad, Mum, Roisin and I moved from England to Ireland. I left friends and family behind but still remain in contact with them, although during my life sadly my Grandad Cyril passed to the spirit world.

We stayed with my Dad's parents in Monasterboice, known to many as Mick, (pops to his family) and Kitty McGahon, for a while, until my Dad and Mum got a house. I got to know a lot about Dad's family. In my Grandparent's house also lived my uncle, who I started to look upon as an older brother. My Dad comes from a family of eleven, we are a very close family, and all of us are always there for each other. Grandad Mick would sit with me each morning, while Mum and Dad were out, we would have boiled eggs, which Granny Kitty made. During the day, our uncle gave me bowls of beans until Mum came back and made dinner for us. To this day, I don't really like beans, perhaps I've had my fill!, I'm sure my uncle made other food but the beans stick in my mind. While in my grandmothers she would make delicious homemade bread. I would sit at the table and help her. I valued my time with her, she is a wonderful grandmother and much loved and respected by all our family. She has passed down her values of family through us all, and to this day she is the reason that we are such a large and close family. Granny would always make delicious chicken soup, and make Christmas puddings for all our families at Christmas, and I must say no-one can make chicken stuffing like she can. I enjoyed my Granny and Grandads stories of old. Grandad would tell me all about his work in Drogheda port and the milk runs, all the ghost stories of the area including the banshees. Granny would tell me all about the ballroom dances and the stories of the Black and Tans. After three months, we moved to Duleek, during this time I was aware of Spirit people but to be honest I was so busy going to school and playing with friends I did not take much notice. I was busy fitting in at Duleek. I lived there until I was thirteen, during this time in Duleek my beautiful sister Emma was born and my handsome brother Luke.

Throughout my early days in Ireland, I was brought to mass, I didn't always listen in mass, and like most children I was bored, but understood it was a way that Catholics were to be brought up. I sometimes would question the whole Heaven and Hell thing, as a child Hell terrified me, and to this day I totally believe in God, but do question some aspects of my religion. I also have belief in reincarnation, which is different from my church. I believe that God makes us so unique that we return to earth many times in different forms to experience all different types of lives and emotions, only when we experience all of these, do we sit with God. I believe that the more we reincarnate the more spiritual we become, hence the old saying an "old head on young shoulders". Throughout my life I have been challenged by sceptics, and none believers who like to challenge what I do. I deal with this by accepting and appreciating that we are all entitled to our opinions. I respect their view. In my opinion I believe that sceptics are young spirits whom have not been reincarnated many times, so everything they see may appear black and white, and there is no in-between. I never have or would force my beliefs of spirit on anyone, as we are all individuals and have our own opinions.

BACK TO MONASTERBOICE

My Grandfather Mick was at an auction one day in Monasterboice in order to bid for a site down the road from his house on behalf of my Dad. Although I had enjoyed living with my Grandparents before, I was older now and had made many friends in Duleek. I was now 13 years old and the idea of moving back to Monasterboice, did not appeal to me. For a while in our new home, I felt lonely, as I did not know any of the young people there. My Mum and Dad were understanding, and told me not to fret, that I would soon make plenty of friends. My Grandparents lived up the road from our house, and my uncle was always over in our house. My Grandad would pop over daily to see if there was anything he could do to help with settling in. I would sit in my room listening to music, but I started to become aware of spirit people around me, not really visions or images, but strange smells, my body temperature changing quickly and my hair moving slightly, so this gave me comfort. My Dad drove a minibus for some years, a red and white one with McGahons Mini bus hire wrote on it, which later at the youth club dances you could see coming a mile away. After a while, I joined the Monasterboice Youth Club, and slowly started to make many good friends, some of whom are still in my life today. I remember one youth club disco, Dad came to collect me at 11pm, but the disco was on till 12, I didn't want to leave and was being a stubborn teenager, Dad asked me to get in the bus, but I wanted to stay, Dad threatened to do a handstand in the middle of the disco if I didn't get in the bus, I laughed it off, but he did a handstand. I legged it onto the bus, at the time this embarrassed me, however, it is now something I would probably do with my own children. Dad has always had a great sense of humour, he is easy to talk to and I consider him not just my Dad but also as one of my best friends. There was one particular friend whom I made while in Monasterboice, Michael (Mickey) Floyd. Mickey was a great character, he sorted out people's problems and was the matchmaker in the area, a very happy person and someone I am glad to have met, he helped introduce me to many people and made me more comfortable with the move from Duleek to Monasterboice.

In the early teen years I had to deal with my emotions and body changing, thinking about what I wanted to be when I grew up. Who am I on the inside, what my spirit journey is and trying to fully understand. I realise now we will never fully understand spirit but I had a lot to learn. I Liked changing my appearance a lot, sometimes in mad ways. I remember my Mum told me I couldn't dye my hair blonde, so I got her yellow powder paint and put it in my hair, which was to be a big mistake. I went from trying to be a Madonna look alike, to the gothic stage, long hair, then big baggy jumpers and shaved hair, these were stages of finding myself, although some of the friends I made later in Monasterboice did think I was a bit mad, but yet again they may have been right.

MY SCHOOL

I went to the Sacred Heart School in Drogheda, at that stage it was run by Sister Monica. We had morning assembly everyday for prayers. I used to be bored to honest in assembly and tried to skip it, but always got caught in the locker room with my friend (you know who you are), protecting your identity BOB. Little did I know how important this praying in the morning was and ironically enough, I now pray every morning to God, his angels, and my guides. At first, I thought Sister Monica was a very strict woman, with her one-way system in the corridor, but later realised she was a kind and genuine woman who really cared about her students. After secondary school I went to study to be a secretary, little did I know that this was not a job intended for me, God and his angels had other plans mapped out for me.

While my journey with spirit was not straight forward, at one stage of my life I decided and chose to study to be secretary, I think this was my way of doing something I felt I could be in control of and organised, and that things could be filed and put into their places.

MY OWN FAMILY

At the age of 18 our son Jonathon was born, a whopping 8lb 9oz. This is one of the most special moments in my life; the secretarial studies were thrown aside. I was a Mum now. Motherhood became the most important job to me, and to this day will always be one I constantly treasure. Throughout my life as a mother, one man was and is always there for me, my darling husband and soul mate Johnny.

While I was pregnant with our second son Séan, our family received some terrible news, on the 24th October 1997, that my dear uncle and friend had suddenly passed to spirit world. The whole world came to a standstill for me; I could not believe that he was gone. For a while I was so angry with God, as I watched the pain my Dad, Mum and the whole family were going through.

On the 1st November my husband brought me to the hospital with what I thought were labour pains. I was suffering with severe pains, but after tests were done, I was told that I was not in labour, but they kept me in for observation due to the pain I was experiencing. I had never experienced physical pain like this before, as the birth of our son Jonathon had been okay and the labour pains were bearable. However, suffering these pains over a number of days, I was exhausted. I must say the staff at the Lourdes Hospital in Drogheda were lovely and very attentive; some just came and sat with me when my family had gone home, and talked to me, reassuring me as I was scared.

On the 3rd November, I was so tired I asked my husband to see the doctor and ask about

11

breaking my waters. I really felt I could not do this anymore. I prayed to God and his angels to help me, and that evening before Johnny had chance to speak with the doctors my waters broke while I was in the ward by myself the spirit world had heard my prayers. It was at this moment in time I realised my spiritual abilities and started to understand there was much more to me than meets the eye. I had always been open and shared some of my feelings about the spirit world with my husband, who although had been a personal disbeliever at the time, had always supported me in every way.

On the 4th November, I had my first full clear vision of someone sitting next to me; strangely, it did not frighten me, because it was my loving uncle by my side. The nurses had been informed that my waters had broke; and when they came in to check on me, I told them that I was okay, and that I was sitting talking to my uncle, I asked them would they ring my husband to come in. The nurse looked shocked, concerned and confused at what I had said, and just ran to the phone quickly, and told my husband what I had just said. Johnny told her not to question me and that he would be in shortly.

While waiting for Johnny to arrive I believe my uncle had expanded the hospital bracelet around my wrist and onto my knuckles, and placed his hand softly on mine, this gave me great comfort. We talked for a while; it is a precious moment in my life, I feel that will always be in my memory box. My uncle had come to give me a warning that there would be a complication with Séans birth, but to assure me not to worry, that he would be there for me. My uncle told me that Johnny would have to make a decision on something, and that Johnny was to shout the word vacuum when the problem happened. When Johnny arrived, my hospital bracelet snapped and my uncle was gone. It did not sadden me, as I knew I would see him again and I did. I told Johnny about the conversation I had had with my uncle, Johnny reassured me that everything would be okay, but in my heart I knew my uncle would be right, and also there for me.

Some hours later, when the birth was close, my heartbeat and our son's heartbeat had been lost on the monitor. As I had taken gas, my poor husband was asked to make a decision for me to have a vacuum birth, as all of this was happening, commotion around me, in the corner of the room I saw my uncle smiling at me. Johnny decided on the vacuum and a big thanks to God and my uncle our son Séan was born healthy, and without any further problems with Sean, to this day I am so grateful.

However, after the birth, my temperature went very high, fans were placed all around me to help cool me down. Doctors and nurses were running all around me. It is hard to explain but I believe I half travelled to the spirit world. I spoke to my uncle, thanking him for his help and advice during Séans birth, then he told me, "Tara it's not your time, you have lots of work on earth to do", suddenly my temperature dropped to normal and I felt peaceful and contented. Little did I know this whole experience was to be the start of my life as a medium, and helping to contact the spirit world to help others.

LIFE IN CLOGHERHEAD

We were living in Clogherhead at this time, after moving there in 1997. We were busy getting on with our lives and looking after our two sons, and settling into the village. I still kept contact with friends from Monasterboice, especially Mickey, who was my husband's best friend. When my sons' were a little older, I got a job in the kitchen of the local pub, The Harbour Bar; I worked with Noel and Marian, the two Ann's and Charlene. I got to know many of the locals.

My sister Emma told me she had made an appointment with a medium and asked would I like to go with her, so I did. I had started feeling "strange" things again, and my visions of the spirit people had begun to reappear. I was excited, but slightly apprehensive as to what the medium would tell me. I wondered whether my Grandfather Mick (Pops) would make contact with the medium for me, he had travelled to spirit a while after my uncle. The reading I had with this woman left me with a lot to think about, she had asked me why I did not work with spirit and told me in detail the visits and visions I had experienced and those which I would have. The medium told me that I would end up reading for people, and I too would become a medium, and making a difference in these people's lives. I told friends about what she had said, and they did not seem shocked, as I expected them to. I told a friend of mine Ann-Marie, and one day she arrived back from Dublin with a set of Tarot Cards for me.

To be honest, in the beginning I just started mucking around with them, not realising how powerful they are. I was always drawn to a particular pattern with the cards that I believe that Brendan showed me. Later, when I researched the pattern, I found it to be an ancient Vietnamese spread. At first I only read the cards for friends, but then as time went on, as my readings became stronger and more accurate, more people started coming to me, as they had been told by others whom I had read for previously. I was amazed, and still am at the belief people have in me. I began to have strange dreams and connecting in dreamtime with spirit people, premonitions and predictions, I found this a little scary at first but I believe it to be part of my continuous journey of discovery.

During my dreamtime, I believe that we switch off our conscious mind and accept what we sense and see. This for me is when spirit people can communicate with us without questioning. One particular dream comes to mind. I have changed the names to protect the person I have read for.
One Wednesday night, a young man appeared to me in my dream, I had met him several months previously, before he had passed, he did not believe in mediumship at the time. He came to me laughing in my dream at the fact that he wanted me to pass on his message. Daniel had suffered from drug addiction on earth, and his death was put down to an overdose of his addiction. Daniel, explained in detail the truth of his passing, and said he would bring his mother to me, that she was not doing so well, he gave me details of memories he had with her, as proof he had visited me. I woke to the sound of a text message on my phone. It was a text message requesting an appointment for Daniels mother. I replied, asking for her to visit in three days time. I wrote down the messages I got from Daniel, so I wouldn't forget. Daniels Mum arrived I didn't use

the cards with her, We talked for a long time and she confirmed the information and details I had given her, most of the message was of reassurance from her son, and she found these messages a great comfort. I remain friends with this woman to this day and am glad to have a chance to help her in her grief. Any spirit people, who come to me, have never had pain. I don't believe that human pain travels to the spirit world, this may seem strange but I believe when we get to spirit, we leave the pain in the body we were born in, and are free in spirit to be with their loved ones on earth. The hardest pain and grief I experienced was someone very close to me that has travelled to the spirit world and whom had decided to cross themselves over. I found this very difficult to come to terms with, but my belief in the spirit has helped me lots and I know they are at peace.

MY MEDIUMSHIP

One night I had a dream about my guide
Brendan; we had been talking at a crossroads.
He told me it is about time I work fully with spirit,
and connecting with them. I asked him how I
would do this properly, he just said trust in me
and I will show you. The next evening I had a
reading. I prepared myself by meditating, and
asking for guidance from Brendan, My uncle and
my Grandfather in spirit. Deep down I knew I
had to say what my 'gut feeling' told me, and
what senses I felt or visions I saw as I read. I was
very nervous before the woman came, but even
now, I am always nervous before I start, but
Brendan tells me that what makes me humble for
what spirit gives me and who I am. I believe the
spirit world is solely responsible for my work and
there is no room for ego (Edging God Out) in my
life.

When the woman arrived, I was aware of a shiver
coming over me and a smell of chestnuts, which I
had learned this was Brendan's way of telling me
he is with me. I was ready for our work to begin.
I asked the woman to turn the cards accordingly,
as she turned them, her eyes dulled, and a
shadow appeared over her right shoulder. Over
time, I have come to realise the eyes are the
windows of the soul and can tell a lot about a
person. I started to tell her about this man over
her right shoulder. I detailed his character as
Brendan told me, his facial features become
clearer. I went onto tell her it was her father. I
heard Brendan give me a name and I blurted it
out. The lady confirmed it was her father's name,
so I continued, trying not to become shocked with
myself but feeling good about what I had told her.
The woman's Dad had crossed to the spirit world

from cancer, six years ago. I found myself going into understanding her emotions, as I seem to do with most of my readings, as cancer was what my grandfather (Pops) had crossed over from. I paused and held her hand to comfort her, as the reading went on I assured her that her Dad was in no pain in the spirit world and brought forward many happy detailed memories of her and her father in the past, as the reading was coming to an end her father touched my head softly and thanked me. It was an amazing feeling and one words cannot describe. This woman remains in contact with me to this day and says I have brought great comfort to her in her life, of which I am truly honoured to be part of. After the woman left, Brendan told me how proud he was of me and that I will learn many more things in time.

The next morning I was so excited about what had happened and went straight up to Mum's to tell her about my experience. She always understands, she sat back and smiled and said "finally you have accepted this gift". My Mum was always a bit psychic. I recall an instance when we moved back to Monasterboice new neighbours moved into a house behind ours, and before even meeting them she already told my Dad their names. Mum always seemed to do things like that, often to the amazement of others. A week after my experience with the woman, Mum and I went to see a medium who told Mum she was a healer and a spirit artist. This pleased me a lot, now we were even more alike as if two peas in a pod. We could now work together like Brendan told me. I was excited about our work in the future. Mum always put me first, and did not always believe she had the gift of healing. However, I have always believed in Mum, and knew she was a healer 100%. We talked a lot about our beliefs in spirit and our enjoyment of our work around this. Mum mentioned her conversation about healing to one of her art students, the woman had a medical issue and asked would Mum practice her healing on her.

The woman described how she had begun to experience a warm tingling feeling as Mum placed her hands above her head, Only then did Mum begin to believe in herself. Like me, gradually through word of mouth, Mum's abilities were shared from one person to another. Many people praise the difference she has made in her work, and will continue to go to her for her healing. My Mum is the humblest person with the gift of healing I have ever met, and I continue to learn from her.

My Mum has taken pen to paper - here in her own words.

"How do I start to explain something I don't fully understand myself? About five or six years ago, 2004 – 2005 I was told by a medium that I was a very powerful healer, I found it mildly amusing at the time, and thought no more about it until one day when I was teaching an art class. I got talking to one of the women there who had recently undergone surgery on her back. She told me that since the operation she had lost the feeling in one of her legs. It was numb from the knee down. One thing lead to another, and I told her what the medium had told me. She didn't hesitate and asked me could she be my first guinea pig. So thinking I had nothing to lose by trying, I simply held my hands over her leg, closed my eyes, and prayed to God that he would use me as a channel for healing. I called upon angel Raphael, the healing angel, and my spirit

19

guide Agupta to pray with me for healing. When I did this I saw a white light in front of my closed eyes, and continued to pray until the white light disappeared. When I asked if anything had happened, she told me she had felt a heat surge through her leg, and a throbbing in the sole of her foot. It took me a while to realise that she really meant it. I was totally gobsmacked. But it gave me the confidence to try to help others. Since that day the healing has got stronger and stronger, some say they feel cold, some say they feel as if they are being prodded, others feel totally relaxed and sleepy. I don't take on the pain of my patients, but I do know when the healing is working, as I get prolonged sweats. This must have something to do with the energies, which I must admit I don't fully understand. I don't know why I have this gift, but I do know it was given to me to help as many people as I can, which I hope I do, the only other reason is that I do believe one hundred percent in the afterlife, and fully believe in the work my daughter and I do with our guides".

EMOTIONS

In my life, I have suffered depression, and I am not ashamed to say it. Depression is very real and can take control. I do hope that you the reader will accept that I wish to keep the reasons for my depression private. However, I will say it was due to a decision I made in my life, which in hindsight I would probably not choose to take again. In spite of this, the path I took and the pain I experienced I believed was part of my learning and growth. I did survive and out of the darkness I gained something which I can and will treasure for the rest of my life. While my family were supportive of me at this stage in my life. I believe I had to help myself. At first, I thought if I went to a counsellor, it would be something I would be embarrassed to say. For a long time I thought about it, and then one day thought, if I broke my arm I would go to a doctor and get it fixed, so if I cannot deal with my emotions I go to a counsellor and that was just it. I took myself off to a counsellor, my Mum came with me, sitting outside in case I needed her, this was one of the best decisions I had made. The counsellor helped me get through this hard time in my life and showed me many ways to get through my depression. Little did I know, that in time, I would be able to help people who came to me, to do the same, but then again it was part of the plan that the spirit world had for me. Since this I have experienced, happiness, love, sadness, grief, joy and many more emotions. Sometimes I feel that my life is like a jigsaw puzzle, getting piece by piece as time goes on. To date I have continued connecting spirit and reading for many people. Each time I read I love to meet these new and interesting people. Although I never remember their readings, as Brendan clears them from my head when I am finished.

One day something happened which made me realise that I really needed to seek help with my depression. The day was not unlike any other, I was out shopping with my son in Tesco's. Suddenly, something triggered a memory of what had caused my depression, I started to panick, not knowing what was coming over me, I burst out in tears, I picked up my son, left the trolley and headed to the door. I ran to my car, locking both my son and myself in side I cried for an hour, it seemed so much longer. This experience scared me so much, but enough to know I needed help. Later when I started counselling I was to find out that what I had experienced was a panick attack. I had pushed emotions and feelings down and they had come to the surface. To anyone going for counselling I would say stick it out for at least 10 sessions. (even now if I am feeling a little down I go for a 'top up', although thankfully it has been a number of years since I was feeling that low). I have learned that crying when releasing emotions is not a weakness but something that makes you strong.. Have you ever noticed that a good cry and sleep helps, you wake up and have this little extra inner strength to deal with the next day, even though the same issues that upset you may still be there. I believe when we sleep the angels and our spirit guides help heal us, and sometimes in our dreams give us options and answers to our emotional problems.

By Sylvia McGahon

Angel Poem

Angels protect you wherever you are
To me they are my sparkling star
When Angels spread out their wings to fly
They seem to light up the sky
Angels guide you under their wing
Listen carefully and you might hear them sing
They're eyes change colour like no other
They're eyes sparkle and glisten in the sky
Angels to me mean a lot and are the best thing
ever
It is the best to find Angels feather

By Leanne Coyle
(My beautiful daughter)

ANGELS IN MY LIFE

One evening, about a year ago, as I was going to bed, I started to see beautiful colours on my bedroom wall, this happened several times. A woman called to the door one morning after this and gave me a beautiful gift of an angel book for the help I had given her some time back. I was surprised and very touched at her thoughtfulness. I started to read this book and linked it to the colours of the angels, blue and pink at this time were the normal colours I had seen on the wall. I recognised these colours of Archangel Michael, the protector of people. I started to read more about Archangel Michael and prayed to him. I could feel extreme cold as I spoke with him, I believe Archangel Michael to be a very powerful angel, later in my readings he had become my angel who worked with me in white light and positive energy.

As I was getting ready to work one evening on my readings and medium ship with my guides, I became very much aware of Archangel Michael, it was as if my face was being touched by white feathers softly, I asked him if everything was okay, he told me that he was there to protect me, that there was something I would be shown, but to trust he was there for me. Four ladies arrived that evening, the first three ladies I read for had beautiful connections, the fourth came in, all of a sudden I felt sick to the stomach and got a bad headache, but I continued to sort the tarot cards, as the lady turned the cards, they did not make any sense to me, so I had to tell her in a polite way that I didn't think I could read for her, she got up from the table and verbally abused me in a way I had never experienced before, this was a learning process for me, to understand that I cannot read everyone, and to remain humble when this happens. I politely asked the woman to leave, while still shaking from the experience; the other people apologised for her behaviour and took her home.

I stopped reading for six months although people asked me to read for them. I started to question myself a lot, and began to read many books about spirit workers. At this time I thought that I controlled whether I wanted to read or not, but found as I continued on my journey that the spirit world can only make this decision.

One morning, I decided to go into town to do shopping. I met a woman I had read for about a year previously called Elaine. Although I hadn't remembered her reading she called my name from across the road, I went over and she started to laugh, and said it was all my fault. Confused, I asked what did this mean, Elaine started to explain, and said at her last reading with me, I had told her that the next time I would see her, she would be five months pregnant, and coming back from a scan at the hospital, and after finding out that she was having a baby boy. She said that she was indeed five months pregnant, had just left the hospital after having her scan, and the baby was a boy. It shocked me, I was pleased for her, offered my congratulations, but that the pregnancy was not my fault! We chatted for a while and I went on my way shopping. This was to be confirmation of my work.

In my dreams, I had begun to get messages and predictions again. I woke one morning with the feelings of both happiness but dread, I couldn't understand. The dream indicated that I would get a phone call that day, and that maybe I needed to

think about starting to read the cards again.
Indeed an hour later, a woman rang me and I
asked her to come and see me that evening. I
spent a lot of time that day asking my guides to
help me conquer my fears. The woman (I shall
call her Jane) arrived at 8.30pm, and I began to
read, her emotional thoughts came through, both
negative and positive, First I thought that it was
strange, it was as if I had not taken a break at
all. The details and spirit messages came in
clear, Jane thanked me after her reading and
left. I thanked my spirit guides for the reading. I
was back on track.

Early the next year, 2000 my beautiful daughter
Leanne was born, my life was now becoming
busier, and however, I continued my work with
spirit with a lot of help and support from my
husband. A couple of years went by as I
continued to read and work with spirit alongside
with my wonderful Mum when she could be with
me when she was not teaching art.

I was glad that I was able to overcome the
negative feelings about my work. I believe
negative feelings are a frame of mind, we can
either let it build up, by thinking and not talking
about what bothers us, if we share our feelings as
I did with my counsellor, its enlightening. We cry
and then talk, and at the end of it we can cope.
To this day if I feel negative emotions like anger,
jealousy, feeling low, or just feeling out of place. I
will talk it through. If there is no-one around, I
would write my feelings down, probably cry as I
do so. Then 'I dust myself down and get on with
it'. This always helps bring positive energy back.
Sounds mad but it works. I believe we can
achieve anything we want in life if we just keep
that positive energy there. The negative energy

only puts obstacles there. We only have this lifetime to be who we want to be, so why waste time on negative stuff. Surround yourself with positive energy, positive people and live life to the full, overcome all obstacles as we come across them.

RACHEL

In March 2005, our fourth child was due to be born. Rachel was due to be born in the last week of the Month. Mum and I were still working together and started to realise that during our work we had become telepathic with each other, we understood each other without speaking, on several occasions we had predicted things for each other in the future that have come through. One sense of our telepathy became very real as my daughter Rachel was being born, and at this time yet again at our Childs birth, my spirit guides were there to help.

At the beginning of March my Dad and Mum had taken a trip to South Africa, they would be back in time for the due date of our daughter Rachel, what they did not realise is that Rachel had plans to arrive early. My labour pains started two weeks early, as my parents were in Africa. At 10.35am on the 9th March my Mum turned to my Dad and said we are too late, Tara has given birth, and Mum had experienced what she describes as a warm feeling in her abdomen and a fluttering of joy in her heart. Dad took my Mums prediction to mind, my husband rang my parents in Africa shortly after and confirmed that Rachel had been born at exactly 10.35, as Mum had said; this is exactly how things have developed between Mum and I.

Rachel's birth seemed to be a normal one up until just before her delivery, while on the gas and pain relief I was convinced my husband told me to push faster, although after the birth he insists he never did, as he did not know there was a problem at the time. I later found out that Rachel was born with the cord around her throat, if I had continued at the normal pace I might not have her. These voices I believe to have been my spirit guides, perhaps Brendan, my uncle or my grandad or all combined. But I know 100% it was not a person in the room to tell me to push harder as there was a problem, as no-one sensed there was one. I am so grateful for my spirit guides in my life and value my family above everything. On coming home from hospital I took some time out to spend with my family, knowing how lucky I am. It is through some experiences I have learned the value of life, it is not what we own or what assets we have that matter, it is the people and love that we are surrounded by. Material things are not so important.

It wasn't until the September of that year, when Rachel was six months old, that I started to read cards again, I met many lovely people and to this day appreciate them sharing their lives with me. During this time of reading and working with Mum I learned many different ways spirit people connect with me, too many to mention but will try to elaborate in the next chapter.

As I have said earlier, Mum had sensed Rachel's early birth, there were many more predictions after this from Mum, one was the case of a car accident.

One Tuesday morning, I went up to Mums for a cuppa, as I like to do at least twice a week. Mum had said she'd had a really bad nightmare, and was disturbed by the vision. Mum dreamt she was in a car accident, the car she had been travelling in had been hit badly by a red car, she had heard a really loud bang that had woke her, she kept thinking, im okay, im okay. I reassured her that this was just a nightmare, we had coffee and chatted and I returned home.

Some Months later, My husband and I planned our first holiday with our family to Bulgaria. There was great excitement in our house, we were to set off at 4am on an early flight on a Monday morning. We had never been on a sun holiday as a family before, so the kids were running round getting swimsuits, packing bags for themselves, all of which I had to repack of course. They were bringing everything but the kitchen sink. Johnny had taken holidays from work for two weeks, Friday to Friday. So the Saturday before we were due to leave for Bulgaria on the Monday, we decided to go out and have a few drinks in town. We ordered a taxi and got ready. The taxi arrived at 9pm. We drove towards town, as we were approaching the petrol station, known to many as the Jet, a car came around the S bend on the other side of the road, under the bridge. The driver was drunk driving, my pet hate, I was sitting in the back of the taxi, my husband in the front. I was just commenting on the other cars erratic driving, then suddenly bang, the loudest bang I have ever heard, everything became blurred, I could see smoke coming from the front of the taxi, the taxidriver was shouting to get me out, while recalling this and writing it, I feel very emotional at the memories of this, as they are still somewhat clear. I remember seeing my husband crawling out of the car, desperately trying to get me out of the back of the car. I was thinking about my kids, and some strong memories flooded into my mind. I suddenly remembered Mums vision of the car accident. I started thinking, im okay, im okay. I looked and indeed the other car was red. This all happened in slow motion, the drunk driver and his two mates were running down the road away from the accident, they didn't care whether we were dead. I was in shock that any human could do this. This driver as I said had been drunk, he had clipped the path and left the ground and landed down on our taxi. I thank God that my husband and the taxi driver were ok. They came to my door, I was told that the taxi had spun around and I had been thrown about in the back. I had my seatbelt on, which had definitely saved my life. The back door opened my husband opened my seatbelt, they linked me under both arms and brought me to safety. I felt my legs had been lifted, although no-one had lifted them. The feeling of "im ok" stayed with me, as the lovely lady from the petrol station got me a drink. At this time the taxidriver had radioed into fellow drivers to look for these three drunken men who had fled the scene of the accident. A large crowd had gathered, the fire brigade and ambulance had arrived quite quickly. The smoke from the taxi was dealt with. As I was sitting I burst into tears, I was alive and Mums vision was with me. Johnny rang Mum and Dad to tell them what had happened. Dad was very worried, and Mum came to the phone, asking Johnny was it a red car, Johnny answered yes, Mum told Johnny I would be okay, she just knew it. We were taken to the hospital, the taxi driver and Johnny were allowed home after tests showed no major injuries. However, the hospital insisted on keeping me in, as I was complaining of neck and abdomen pains, and was severely bruised across my body, you could see the line of where the seatbelt had held me.

I couldn't believe what had happened. My whole family came in immediately. I was more upset for the kids, our holiday to Bulgaria was on Monday, would I be out, would we go? It was now Sunday and I had to undergo x-rays and scans. I have never prayed so hard to be okay. I couldn't let my kids down, they were so excited about their holiday. We hadn't told them what had happened, we didn't want to frighten them. Johnny told them I had stayed in a friends house. Meanwhile the drunk drive had turned himself in. Perhaps the guilt took over of what he had done, or perhaps he was still drunk and didn't know what he was doing. I have learned not to hate this man, perhaps what happened was to teach him about his behaviour in endangering himself and others, a lesson, I pray he has learned from it.

The x-rays and scans came back clear, I was allowed to go home at six oclock that Sunday evening. But I was told I would probably have a lot of pain with my bruising, and maybe going on holiday was not a good idea, so me being me, and loving my family so much, got on the plane with my kids and husband and went to Bulgaria that Monday morning. When we arrived in Bulgaria, the sun was splitting the stones as the Irish would say. We went to the hotel and got something to eat and went to our rooms. We slept for a while, as all of us were tired. In the afternoon we prepared to go to the pool. I went to the balcony of the room, which was overlooking the pool, all the other holidaymakers were down, sunning themselves at the pool, I was thinking that most of them had beach perfect bodies, and there was me covered in bruises, I really didn't want to go down. I sat for a while and thought what I look like on the outside is not as important as who I am on the inside. At times people can be superficial, will concentrate and judge others on their outside appearances, and are unaware that it is what is on the inside that counts and of more importance. I went slowly down the pool, with my kids, I had told them that the bruises were from a fall I had the day before. I was aware that a number of people stopped and stared, how could I arrive at the pool like this?. I went in the pool, but movement in the water was hard, I was stiff and very sore. When I saw my kids laughing and having fun, it didn't matter about my appearance and soreness. Johnny called me and said he had a surprise for me. He had spoken to the person doing massage at the side of the pool, and explained what had happened. Johnny said he had booked me in for a massage for each of the days that we would be there. Johnny is a very kind hearted loving man, and i'm so happy that he is my husband, we had a great holiday, and one I will never forget.

WHAT IS MEDIUMSHIP TO ME

I am honest as a medium; I do not always see spirit people, when I read it is not what my work is solely about. I believe each and every one of us who have an open mind can feel, sense, smell or see our spirit people. We all have this ability within, spirit connect with us on a daily basis but sometimes we are too busy to notice. During this book I have purposely not written down in details names of people I have read for, as each reading is private, as I connect it can be something simple like a song I hear and speak of, a thought or a feeling I have, a smell or sometimes a visual. I hope by writing this book to encourage people to realise that spirit people and angels are always around and at the end of it all, it is my belief God is our boss.

Mediumship is about helping people deal with grief. I believe my readings are ones of comfort and guidance. I don't have any 'bad cards' in my pack. I only work in the light of God, and that is one of love and purity. One of the most powerful readings I have been given permission to write about, and of a truely inspirational and amazing woman, and a huge credit to her family, Sharon McKey.

One morning around ten, I got myself a coffee and sat at my laptop. Onto facebook I went. I read all and chatted. A lady called Sharon who I had never met or read for sent me a message of grave concern. Sharon apologised for contacting me, but did not know where to turn. Everything in her life was hard, she had cancer, she was tired, and felt the only option was to end her life. She was worried that she was a burden to her family, although she stressed that they were always there

for her and a great support. I didn't know why
Sharon chose to tell me, and she said she had
told no-one else how she was feeling. I asked this
lady for her phone number. I believed it was a
cry for help. I didn't know how I could help, but
felt that I needed to talk to her face to face.
Sharon sent me her number. I rang her
immediately as I felt timing was important. I
asked her if she had a form of transport, I would
like to see her straight away for a chat. We
organised a time to meet, and asked her not to
end her life, and would she be willing to at least
give me a chance to help. Sharon promised not
to do anything before we met. To be honest, I
was very scared. I didn't know how to help this
emotionally burdened lady. I prayed and prayed
for support off my guides, and told Mum about it.
Mum told me to go with my gut feelings. The next
day came and Sharon arrived with tears in her
eyes. I hugged her at the door, I could feel her
pain, and told her to come in for tea! Sharon said
she would love a reading and asked if she could
pay me the following week, I felt this was a slight
shift in how Sharon may be feeling, as she was
planning ahead, which is positive. I told her that
money was not an issue, and if I could help her
that was enough payment for me. I thought
about taking my cards out, and suddenly felt on
this occasion I did not need cards. I became very
much aware of a woman spirit with me. I could
see her visually in my mind. She had other
people with her. I asked Sharon was it okay to
leave the cards and just do mediumship, as it felt
right. She was okay with this. As I described
and felt this spirit woman around me, I was
aware that this was Sharon's mother, I gave
Sharon more and more details as Sharon cried
and confirmed them and that it was definitely her
mother. As the mediumship continued, I became

aware of her Dad beside her Mum, along with two of Sharon's siblings, the emotional pain I felt for her was unbearable, but I had to continue. Both her brothers in spirit came forward with their names, Paul and Malachy. They had crossed at the age of 39 with a year between them. Sharon had a hard life and these losses were too much for her to bear, she had given up on fighting cancer. We cried together as her emotions really affected me. Her spirit people gave even more details and huge encouragement to their daughter and sister Sharon. After the mediumship, we dranks loads of tea and chatted. Sharon promised to keep in contact, saying that taking her own life was not an option she was considering anymore. Sharon contacted me later that week to tell me that she had contacted doctors and was going to fight cancer all the way, as through my mediumship she knew that her spirit people and others were there to help. Sometime ago, Sharon underwent a very scary operation, while staying in contact with me. I'm so proud of her. Sharon had the cancer removed, and was growing stronger and stronger each day.

Sharon had promised to build up her life again. At this time I made a promise to her that I didn't know if I could keep. I promised her that I would get her a private reading with the International Medium Colin Fry, whom she had watched over and over on the television and greatly admired. At this point Colin Fry did not know whom I was, I contacted Colin via facebook explaining to him all about Sharon, not thinking for one minute that I would get a reply. I waited, all the time praying to my guides, Colin wrote back saying that my message was so heartfelt, he would be honoured to meet my friend when he was in Dublin on the 5th November 2010, in the Helix after his show. I was so excited I immediately rang Sharon, she said it was like 'winning the lotto'. As soon as the tickets went on sale I bought them. When the day came, I too was excited about meeting Colin in person, as he has always inspired me as a medium. Sharon, my friend Heather and me went along to the show, and we were ready to meet Colin. The show was amazing, afterwards when we went to meet Colin, I must say the first thing I noticed about Colin was how down to earth, caring and genuine he is. He talked to Sharon for some time, the delight in her eyes was amazing to see, she was shining in positive energy. At the end of the night as we drove home, Sharon talked and talked about the evening all the way home. I felt so happy inside to see Sharon on cloud nine. We had a cup of tea with Sharon before we left to go home.

As I turned to wave goodbye to Sharon and was walking back to the car, I saw a number four over her head, I didn't know why. As Heather and me were driving back home I mentioned this to her, I felt a bit sad as I thought that the cancer would come back in four years. I pushed this to the back of my mind as all that mattered was that Sharon was on top of the world at that moment, and that's all that mattered. I continued to do readings with people for the next while. Still keeping in contact with Sharon, who mentioned the evening with Colin every time we spoke.

Four weeks after meeting Colin, I received a phone call which broke my heart. Sharon had passed to spirit. Her death was due to natural causes, and unrelated to her cancer. My world seemed to fall apart, even writing this at the moment, the ink is blotted with tears. I couldn't believe it, I remembered the number four I had saw over her head, it had meant four weeks. I wondered why life was so cruel, my only consolation at the time was that the last time I had seen Sharon, she was glowing with happiness, and I thank Colin Fry from the bottom of my heart for helping me make her dream come true.

Over the following few weeks, I took some time to deal with my own pain of Sharon's crossing, and to console her wonderful family, especially her own beautiful daughter Charlene and Sharon's sister Ann-Marie.

Sharon lived in Dundalk. At the time of Sharon's passing over, the weather in Ireland had taken a particular turn for the worst, travel had become difficult and at times treacherous to travel. Due to this I could not, unfortunately attend Sharon's funeral, as the roads were too dangerous to take on the day. I did however, manage to go to Dundalk on the eve of the funeral, for a short time, the journey home, which would normally be around 30 minutes travel, took three hours. I love you Sharon, you are forever in my thoughts, it is comforting to know that I have a beautiful new guide in my life now, all will be revealed.

Sharon was truely an inspiring woman to all, and I believed in time would help many other people who are battling cancer, I had hoped that maybe one day she would have written her own book. Thank you Sharon, you have truely shown me the value of my mediumship and what it is really about, making a difference. Sharon believed I was the reason for the turn of events in her life, but I believed Sharon was, as she had this strength inside all the time. I'm just glad she asked me to help her bring it out, love and light to you Sharon x.

THE LAST FIVE YEARS

Over the last five years, I have continued to do my work with my Mum. During these years, many of other opportunities have come my way. I worked on an investigation with Mike Hirons and the team Paranormal Ulster, in Ross castle, all lovely people. I have been asked to do online and phone readings, which can work, but personally, it is not something I would ever do. I prefer to just do face to face readings, my guides tell me the eyes are the window of the soul, and I need to be with the person to read as spirit connection can be very emotional and I prefer to be there in person to support the people I read for.

Last November I did my first medium ship show live on stage with a colleague of mine medium Declan Flynn. To be honest I was so nervous before the show, as it was without my cards and out of my comfort zone. Nevertheless, the night went great and I was happy. Declan had invited me to join him on stage. The next medium ship show came up for me in June 2010, with my close friends and colleagues Heather Evans and Robbie Andrews. These are two mediums that I know have been and are a great influence in my life. Heather and Robbie, had voted for me to go on stage first. With makeup, hair and new clothes on, I went on stage, the high heels I had on were killing my feet so me being true to myself, introduced who I am, and then asked before I began, would anyone mind if I took off these high heel shoes, im not very tall!, but I needed to be bare footed, strange but I feel more grounded if I read in my bare feet. I started to look around the room, and felt a male spirit on my right, I usually get cold on the righthand side if it is male and on the left side if its female, its just how spirit has shown me. I felt this man was reaching to communicate with a lady to the right of me in the audience, and as I started to describe him, a lady on the right understood who he was. I told her he had been a healthy man, who loved his salads, but didn't like mayonnaise, the lady told me she had prepared food for him many times, salad one of his favourites, and that he did not like mayonnaise. Spirit person, after spirit person came through, and although I had been on stage for half an hour when time was up, it felt like it had only been five minutes I hope to work more with them in the future.

Sometime later I was contacted by a journalist called Martin Grant, a genuine man and a journalist to watch out for in the future, he asked could he interview me and my Mum about the combined work we do, mediumship, cards, healing and telepathy. Martin asked would I mind reading for him, so we met for lunch, Martin, Mum and I. Martin was a lot younger than I thought he would be, but a lovely man, full of ideas and goals, a lovely positive energy about him. The reading for Martin went well, and some spirit details he got confirmed by his family when he went home as they were from an older generation.

At the moment I am continuing to read and work with spirit alongside my Mum, with the great support of my husband and family. Some of my friends have read the drafts of this book, and say i'm too humble for what I do, but that's just the way I am. I couldn't have an ego if I tried. My gift does not belong to me. I am only a channel for spirit people, and my guides and God and his angels are the ones responsible for my work. My friends suggested I put some of the reviews from other people that have been put onto facebook under medium Tara Coyle, so at the the end of my writings are some of the reviews, and a big thankyou to those who had taken the time out to write them.

I also hope to do more mediumships live on stage, so watch this space.

MY LATEST JOURNEY WITH SPIRIT

Over time I continued to do private readings and calling to houses. Also during this time I did a live mediumship evening in McHughs in Drogheda. I must say, when I was doing the live mediumship, I found it to be very nerve racking, standing there while the room is quiet, and everyone there to listen to me.

I feel like I have come a long way with Spirit to date. But my biggest part of the journey so far is to come. Along the way I have been involved with some paranormal investigations with East Coast Paranormal, with lead investigator Mick Doyle for charity. Mick is a lovely guy with a genuine heart, and a great passion for the paranormal. Although I enjoyed working with the team, I believed my own true destiny was to follow my path reading and doing mediumship live on stage.

Over the past year, I had chatted on a few occasions via facebook with Colin Fry. I was delighted to hear that he was again coming to Ireland, and in fact to Drogheda on the 14th April

2011. I immediately bought tickets for Mum and me. A few of my friends had also bought tickets and they too came along the same night. Johnny, my lovely husband, was happy to be at home looking after our children.

Mum and me sat in the audience with excitement as Colin came onto the stage. We enjoyed his show immensely. About half way through his show a lady asked Colin would it be possible to have a private reading with him. Colin said that he would love to read for her but his waiting list had to be cut as there was so many people wanting readings. What happened next, totally blew me away, I was amazed. Colin further explained that although he could not read privately for her, however, the town had an amazing medium which he personally recommended and then he called out my name. I was speechless, (this doesn't happen often!) the camera man Kevin, and manager zoomed the camera in on me. I feel so honoured, that Colin, would speak about me in this way. After the show, people were queuing up to get my number, it was mind blowing. I was excited but in total shock. My Mum was delighted for me, showing it by her big beaming smile. After the que had died down, Kevin, Colin's manager came over to me and said that Colin would like a private word with me, and asked would we be available to meet with him back at the hotel where they were staying, I stood there still in shock, open mouthed and nodded, I wanted to pinch myself to see if this was real. Kevin said that they would follow us along there as soon as Colin had completed his book signing.

I had offered to be the designated driver that evening, and could not even have a drink for the shock, I needed one! Me, Mum and a few of my friends went back to the hotel to wait for Colin to arrive. I waited anxiously, wondering what Colin wanted to speak to me about. Colin arrived about an hour later, we all chatted, the camera flashes went on all around, numerous photographs were taken. Colin then asked could he speak to me in private, my heart was racing, me having a conversation with the fabulous Colin Fry, I felt self conscious, star struck. Colin then asked me, something I could never have ever thought would happen, although it is a dream come true. The 'one and only' Colin Fry asked me would I work with him on one a two shows when he was next doing his shows in and around this part of Ireland. I humbly accepted, finding it hard to take it all in. Another amazing part of my journey was beginning. Over the following few weeks I spoke with Kevin his manager and the dates were set. I was going to be on stage with Colin in Dundalk on the 5th November, its exactly a year and a day from the first time I met Colin in person with Sharon. Now I know that Sharon is over this in spirit. I am also to do another show with Colin on the 7th November in Drogheda. Today, is the 11th of July, 2011, and I have finished my book, I would love this to be published on November 5th in Dundalk on my first appearance with Colin Fry in honour of my friend Sharon.

45

Reviews of my work....

"I watched Tara perform her unique gift in Blackrock, Co Louth at a demonstration of mediumship. Her honest and open heart approach to her work is truly refreshing, inspiring and uplifting. Having received a message on the night myself, I was amazed to her accuracy and detail"
Jacqui McAvinney.

"I have had a reading with Tara. I found her amazing, she told me things on-one else could have known about me. I've had a wonderful experience, she had such wonderful karma about her. Her readings are 100% accurate, she has turned my life around with her gift, her warm heart, her kind spirit"
Eileen O'Rourke.

"I have been to see Tara twice for readings, and both times she was brilliant, she told me things that no-one could have known, and stuff I did not know until after I had visited her. The readings were fantastic, everything she said has come true since then, she is 100% accurate. I think she is fantastic and would recommend her to anyone as I had an amazing experience during my readings"
Lizzy Scully.

"I have been to Tara twice for readings, and found her amazing on both occasions. The readings were very accurate and true. Personal details that nobody else knew about came out in the cards and I really enjoyed the experience. Tara has such a warm and caring personality, and it is always a pleasure to visit her. I would definitely recommend Tara to anyone who is interested in having a reading." Emma Clarke.

Tara done a reading for me a few weeks ago, I've had a great experience since then. A fantastic understanding of some personal stuff that Tara and her guides brought to the surface for me. I got have some personal time with family members who have passed, some amazing tear jerking moments. Tara is a friend during and after the reading, and is at the end of the phone at all times. I've enjoyed my sitting with her, I would recommend it if anyone is thinking of going to a medium, go to Tara Coyle
Shirley Purfield.

Tara is an angel in disguise, from the first day I met her she took me under her wing, she encouraged me and gave me guidance when I didn't know I needed it. She is one of the most caring people I have ever met, and can never repay what she did for me. She saved my life. Love you Taraxx you're the best, its a shame there are only five stars to rate you on facebook
Danny King.

I went to see Tara at a very difficult stage in my life. I was suicidal at the time, she is one of the most amazing people I have ever met. She has qualities very few people have, she put me in touch with my beloved family who assured me they were happy and watching over me all the time. If ever anyone needs reassurance please have an open mind and visit Tara, you will leave feeling like a new person GUARANTEED!!!!!
Sharon McKey

People go to have their readings done for all the right and wrong reasons, but if you have Tara to do it for you, I can assure you that it will be everything and so much more then you will expect.... It will be unforgettable, life changing

47

experience. Tara is an amazing woman, one that I am proud to call my friend! Thank you so very much for being you!!
Natascha Christoph.

"Went to see Tara last night for a reading. I have never had it done before so it was a new experience for me. Tara made me feel welcome and comfortable straight away. The reading was a little personal, so I will just say it works and in my opinion Tara is the real deal, and I would recommend anybody interested in the spirit world to visit her"
Anthony Carolan.

"I have just had my second reading with Tara, she is a wonderful person and an amazing medium. She instantly makes you feel welcome, relaxed and comfortable! She really hit the nail on the head for me and like others Im feeling much more positive and like a weight has been lifted. She doesn't beat around the bush, and gets straight to the issues which are important and relevant to you in a very caring, compassionate and understanding way! Thanks Tara for a brilliant reading, im already looking forward to coming back for more readings in the near future"
Naomi O'Dowd.

"I couldn't believe what Tara was telling me last week. It was a great reading from her. I appreciate her time and for giving me a reading"
Karen Walsh.

"Very good Tara your after spooking me, really pleased with my reading"
Leanne Rooney.

"My friend introduced me to Tara and she arranged a reading for me. I had been to other psychics but neither compared to the warm, comfortable feeling of when I went to Tara. I was so relaxed and the reading was brilliant. My baby daughter who passed over less than a year ago came through to Tara, and I really needed to hear what she was telling me. Tara is gifted, I got so much comfort and reassurance from what she said to me. She told me things she couldn't have known and you know as soon as she starts talking with you that she is honest and it makes a difference. Tara has a very special gift and I thank her so much for sharing it with people. She brings so much peace of mind that many of us need from time to time. Thank you so much Tara for being you"
Donna Molloy.

I got my reading done by Tara for the first time. I was nervous, but once you get talking to Tara she makes you feel soooo comfortable and relaxed :D Tara's works that she does is fantastic as a medium who else would I want in the future as she is spot on when she does her readings. As Tara was doing me reading I felt I had a bit of weight off my shoulders and felt more happier with myself thanks Tara xxxxx
Donna Bracken.

"Tara Coyle Medium, when we hear the word 'medium' we think 'Oh God' what will I hear? Will I hear anything? Well I seen this lady in Blackrock, Co Louth a few months back. To be honest, I was curious to this lady's attunement to the spirit world. That fine fitnesse that one requires or develops within their lifetime, this lady opened up the evening in a relaxed and informative way of how she works. It then

progressed into spirit communication, as she knew her recipient and went straight to them, giving them concise and accurate information of loved ones in spirit. I have seen mediums on mainland Uk, and the standard over there is on par with Tara's demonstration, accurate, soulful, meaningful, beautiful, emphasising we cannot die, we just become tomorrow, thanks Tara"
Adrian T McGrath.

Thanks for the reading Tara, you definitely have a gift have been going over it and there is no way anyone could be that accurate, true gift, thanks again already looking forward to going back
Rosie Power

Absolutely brilliant, told me things she nor nobody else could now, recommended by my aunty who she read, and was well worth the visit, not only did I feel at peace at what she told me but the minute I left her house I felt so much at peace with my life and the troubles that lead me to her. Thank you Tara
Yhana Byrne

Had a reading with Tara such a lovely down to earth person and god she is brilliant would recommend her to anyone. She gave me peace of mind about a lot of stuff. And to know my both my parents are together. Love to Tara will get another reading very soon
Rachel O Sullivan

Had the best reading I ever had with you, nobody could of known all that u told me Tara, was amazing, helped me so much in many ways that nobody or nothing else could. I told my niece and she had a reading with you a week later and boy did you help her too, so grateful Tara and will be

back to you for another amazing reading in 6 months, thank you and god bless
Rhonda Byrne

Hi Tara, Thank you so much for the best reading I've had in a long, long time. What you told me, No one else could know. Thank your mum as well for the great healing. Will book you again next year.
Sharon Campbell

Will keep it short and sweet, Tara a huge thank you for the reading you gave me a couple of weeks ago, I was very impressed with you, you told me things that only me and 1 or 2 other people would have known, I definitely would recommend you to anyone considering a reading or looking for a genuine psychic medium, will defo get up to see you again very soon
Peter Walsh

Tara, many thanks for your reading, you gave me great comfort in knowing that my loved ones who have passed over are watching over us....You knew things about them that know one else would know....and yes I got my brother to check his oil it was low......I have read one of the books that you told me to read and I am ready to start my second.....I am certainly more aware that are loved ones are there for us....thanks for the reading, I wish you well in your future and to your lovely family......I definitely will keep you informed if the future bits you tell me come through...xx
Sharon Davis

I started a spirit circle with my Mum, we sit and talk about our experiences and beliefs, we do not teach as we learn from each other. The circle is a none profit one, just bring along a jar of coffee or packet of biscuits, preferably chocolate ones! Lol. It is a group of people interested in spirit. Some of the group don't work with spirit, but want to, so we just share our experiences. I don't teach as I don't believe anyone is qualified enough to teach, only spirit can do this, but this is just my beliefs. The circle has been running for over seven months now, and I enjoy everytime we meet up, the people in it are beautiful people and between us there is a great positive energy and openness to talk freely about spirit and our experiences. My friend Mickey (Michael Floyd) was also a member of this group, and was loved by all for his stories and genuine character.

On the 11th February, my dear friend and member of our spirit circle Michael (Mickey) Floyd went to the Spirit world. I found his passing very hard, and to this day miss him dearly but completely believe he is with his spirit people looking down on me and helping me with my work. A poem written by my friend Nicola Traynor has been printed on the next page in Mickey's memory

'OUR BUD MICKEY'.....BY NICOLA TRAYNOR.

You shone within our lives,
You cared for all you knew,
Your burdens kept inside for only you to view,
You should have told us something,
We would have helped you through,
However, being the gent you were shook all of us from view,
We miss you dearly mate, our bubbly, lovely chum,
We know you are watching near, waiting for us to come,
Mickey's soul departing tore grief from in our hearts,
Look down on us from heaven; we should not be apart,
Good friend we will see you soon,
When the angels come for us,
But in the meantime never forget how much you meant to us,
Your family miss you bud,
They grieve for you each day,
Send down your love to them, day by day by day,
Sleep tight dear friend Mickey,
With angels by your side,
No funny pranks in heaven, on clouds you will ride,
Shine down your light to us,
Till we're right by your side.

Animal Spirit

In my dreams several times I have remembered an eagle. I have seen the eagle coming towards my face. After having this reoccurring dream one morning, I noticed some scratches on my neck, I didn't know where these came from. The dream came back to me many times, after some time I managed to bump into a bio energy healer who did some work on me. She started to tell me about the dreams I was having and spoke of the eagle. At this time I had developed a huge interest in eagles, and was reading about them. I had bought a necklace in Tenerife with a metal panel on it, and printed on it was an eagle. I had been wearing this necklace for a while and the lady told me that the eagle had been trying to take it off me, hence the scratches, as my body was allergic to it, this was blocking spirit communicating with me. She asked me if I felt tired while wearing this necklace. Strangely enough I had. I had learned over time and through meditation that the eagle was my friend and had come to be my animal guide. I have worked with my animal spirit the eagle, and can sense his presence, he gives me inner strength and allows to connect to a stronger level, as for the eagle the sky is unlimited and free. To date I continue to read for people and am looking forward to working with Colin Fry.

STATEMENT FROM COLIN FRY

"Tara Coyle is one of the new generation of psychics who not only has come out of the psychic closet and is developing quite a following in Ireland (and I am sure the rest of the world soon) in November she will be guesting on my "People's Medium Tour, Ireland 2011". I strongly suggest you not only come to see her demonstrate her evolving gift, but read this, her book to see the journey is not always an easy one"
Colin Fry
International Medium

Big hello to all my friends on face book, and thanks for your patience while I write my book. Thank you for taking the time out in your life to read my book, may the angels always walk with you and God Bless, and remember our loved ones are only a thought away.......

Your friend Tara